Fire Engines

by Marcia S. Freeman

Consulting Editor:
Gail Saunders-Smith, Ph.D.

Consultant:
Mark Edelbrock
Fire Fighter
Seattle Fire Department

Pebble Books

an imprint of Capstone Press
Mankato, Minnesota

Pebble Books are published by Capstone Press,
1710 Roe Crest Drive, North Mankato, Minnesota 56003.
www.capstonepub.com

 Books published by Capstone Press are manufactured with paper
containing at least 10 percent post-consumer waste.

Library of Congress Cataloging-in-Publication Data
Freeman, Marcia S. (Marcia Sheehan), 1937–
    Fire engines / by Marcia S. Freeman.
    p. cm.—(Community vehicles)
    Includes bibliographical references and index.
    Summary: Simple text and photographs illustrate fire engines and the equipment
they carry.
    ISBN-13: 978-0-7368-0102-7 (hardcover)
    ISBN-10: 0-7368-0102-2 (hardcover)
    ISBN-13: 978-0-7368-4985-2 (paperback)
    ISBN-10: 0-7368-4985-8 (paperback)
    1. Fire engines—Juvenile literature. [1. Fire engines.] I. Title. II. Series.
    TH9372.F74 1999
    628.9′259—dc21   98-18380

Note to Parents and Teachers

This series supports national social studies standards related to
authority and government. This book describes and illustrates fire
engines and the equipment they carry. The photographs support early
readers in understanding the text. The sentence structures offer subtle
challenges. This book introduces early readers to vocabulary used in
this subject area. The vocabulary is defined in the Words to Know
section. Early readers may need assistance in reading some words and
in using the Table of Contents, Words to Know, Read More, Internet
Sites, and Index/Word List sections of the book.

Printed in the United States of America in North Mankato, Minnesota.
012012   006536CGVMI

Table of Contents

Fire engines are large trucks. Fire engines carry tools for fighting fires. Fire engines go to fires fast.

Fire engines have sirens and flashing lights. Sirens and lights tell people that fire engines are coming.

Fire engines carry long hoses. Fire fighters hook up hoses to water supplies. Fire fighters use hoses to spray water on big fires.

Fire engines carry
fire extinguishers. Fire
extinguishers spray special
chemicals. Fire fighters
use fire extinguishers to
put out small fires.

Fire engines carry ladders. The ladders are different sizes. Fire fighters use ladders to reach high places.

14

Fire engines carry pike poles. Fire fighters use pike poles to tear holes in roofs. The holes let out hot air and smoke.

Fire engines carry big fans. Fire fighters use fans to blow smoke out of rooms. Fires make a lot of smoke.

Fire engines carry air packs. Fire fighters breathe from air packs when there is smoke. Smoke makes air hard to breathe.

Fire engines return to fire stations after fires. Fire fighters clean the fire engines. Fire fighters keep fire engines ready to go to fires.

Words to Know

air pack—a tank of air joined to a mask; fire fighters breathe from air packs when there is a lot of smoke.

fire extinguisher—a holder with water or chemicals inside it; people use fire extinguishers to put out small fires.

hose—a long, bendable tube that carries water from one place to another

ladder—a metal or wood tool that people climb to reach high places

pike pole—a tool with a hook-shaped end used to tear holes in roofs; the holes let out hot air and smoke.

siren—a machine that makes a loud sound

spray—to scatter liquid in fine drops; fire hoses spray water on fires.

Read More

Ready, Dee. *Fire Fighters.* Community Helpers. Mankato, Minn.: Bridgestone Books, 1997.

Saunders-Smith, Gail. *The Fire Station.* Field Trips. Mankato, Minn.: Pebble Books, 1998.

Somerville, Louisa. *Rescue Vehicles.* Look Inside Cross Sections. New York: Dorling Kindersley, 1995.

Internet Sites

FactHound offers a safe, fun way to find Internet sites related to this book. All of the sites on FactHound have been researched by our staff.

Here's all you do:

Visit *www.facthound.com*

Type in this code: 9780736801027

Index/Word List

Word Count: 184
Early-Intervention Level: 10

Editorial Credits
Colleen Sexton, editor; Clay Schotzko/Icon Productions, cover designer;
   Sheri Gosewisch, photo researcher

Photo Credits
Dembinsky Photo Assoc. Inc., 8; Joe Sroka, cover; Jim Regan, 1; John Mielcarek, 12
Image West/Larry Angier, 18
Mike Heller/911 Pictures, 14, 16, 20
Photo Network/Mark Sherman, 6
Unicorn Stock Photos/Scott Liles, 4; Mike Morris, 10